UNEXPECTEDLY IVY

ORDINARY MOM, HARVARD KID

UNEXPECTEDLY IVY

SEBASTIANA DEVINE

Published by Noble Hound Press
An imprint of Noble Hound Publishing
FIRST EDITION

Book Cover and Interior Design by VMC Art & Design LLC

ISBN: 979-8-9921152-3-9

Published in the United States of America

To all our extraordinary fruits (yes, that's right),
Thank you for making the harvest unforgettable.
With love,
Your ordinary roots

TABLE OF CONTENTS

UNEXPECTEDLY IVY

ORDINARY MOM, HARVARD KID

Every tale deserves a toast—bread in the morning, champagne at night.

COCKTAILS BEFORE THE TALES

(WITH ASSORTED NUTS TO FOLLOW)

I n June 2018, my husband and I retired, just a month after our youngest graduated from college. For the first time in nearly 30 years, we weren't rushing toward anything. Finally, peace.

Until it wasn't.

The fear of growing complacent, of sitting still for too long, started to creep in. I knew I had to move, to make, to create. This book is for everyone who's ever wondered if they're doing life right, especially when the silhouette of success is never quite in focus.

We can't all be mountains. Some of us are lakes, reflecting the glory above us. And in that reflection, the long-awaited silhouette comes sharply into view.

*** If you're expecting this tone to continue, DON'T. The rest of this book? Well…let's just say I loosened some nuts and bolts.

This book wasn't born from a life of red carpets or luxurious moments. It came from the unfiltered daily existence most people recognize. It is stitched together by manic mornings, homework harakiris, and deadline dilemmas.

It's a mix of widely accepted and not-so-universally acclaimed parenting methods. Some will make you nod, others might make you go 'huh.' Both are perfectly normal, I promise. This isn't a guidebook. I'm not here to teach you how to live your best life. I'm just here to tell you how I lived mine, and maybe help you feel extra hopeful and lighthearted as you navigate the Momboat.

Most entries are bite-sized chapteritas (yes, it's a made-up word), those narrative nuggets you can pop and savor in one sitting. But a few have grown into generous slices, because sometimes a story needs to be held a little longer.

You can read them in order or hop around like a child on their third juice box. No judgment here...unless you skip the good parts.

So let's get started. You've got 'teritas to munch on, and I've got to prep for cross-examination in case someone lawyers up.

CONFESSIONS JUST OUT OF THE DRYER

This probably isn't the kind of confession you were expecting...thirty years ago, I might've had something juicier (diagrams and all). For now, you're just getting words—and your imagination (the art comes later, but spoiler: those are mine too).

These pages are left unedited, like a pile of maternal (and the occasional paternal) laundry straight from the dryer: unapologetic in their wrinkles, yet hopeful that someone out there will nod and say, "same." And for those who don't? Hope your clothes steamer brings you joy.

Yes, I wrote. Yes, I painted. And no, I won't narrate the audiobook. Not yet, anyway.

So here are my words in their natural state: some will stumble, some will soar, some will drift toward parenting's sunset...until the waves roll the grandkids in, surfboard and all.

An 8,000-mile trip became
a lifetime journey, proof that
a one-way ticket can circle
the globe and land you where
you need to be.

MAMA FROM MANILA

I grew up with my two younger sisters in a normal middle-class household. Life was simple, and came served with unlimited rice...and a tangy side dish of ambition.

While my sisters were still under my parents' scholarship program, I graduated with a degree in Management at 19. And a couple of months later, landed my first job as Cosmetics and Perfumery Manager at a department store. The only thing I truly managed was not rolling my eyes. So when two friends swore advertising was fun, I thought I'd upgrade. Well, they lied.

Life, as it tends to do, threw in a few plot twists. Three months after I arrived in New York, I was teaching business courses and English as a Second Language in the Bronx and Queens: guiding others toward their path while still stumbling along my own.

When I got pregnant with our youngest child, I took a real break. I became a full-time mom to three kids, which sounded simple enough until I realized there was no HR department.

Eventually, I went back to work albeit part time as a dental assistant. Not quite the glamorous career twist I'd imagined, but the hours allowed me to be mom and moonlight as the Tooth Fairy.

Then I thought I was ready for something bigger. That landed me at a pediatrician's office. Why stop at gums and teeth when you can go viral? There I met Mr. Cold and Mrs. Flu: the notorious power couple.

Ooh, I almost forgot. I likewise dipped into real estate and ended up swimming laps for twenty years. I learned that some people were serious about buying a house, and others thought open houses were a low-cost weekend family outing. My creativity was tested when I had to explain why sellers made logic-defying decisions like wall-to-wall carpeting in the bathroom or a random toilet sitting proudly between the washer and dryer in the basement.

The real estate euphemism list became my survival kit:

Cozy = too small for your mother-in-law to live with you

Loads of privacy = no DoorDash deliveries

Needs TLC = property screams YOLO (You'll Own Lingering Odors)

After a career hopscotch like that, no wonder my high school yearbook labeled me a Jill of all trades—and paradoxically, a master of all. Did my friend who wrote it get it right?

Every dad drives his regular route, but a detour is never off the table.

DAD FROM DA BRONX

My husband was born in the Morris Park section of the Bronx to an Irish family. When he got his 23andMe results, they came back 99% made with Irish parts, fully assembled in the USA. No leprechaun surprise there. Somehow, he was crushed. He clung to that exotic 1% wherever it was …probably lost among his freckles.

He was born to an older set of parents by medical, cultural, and judgmental standards. His dad was 13 years older than his mom, which meant that when he was born, his father was already 53. Thankfully, his dad had the kind of great hair that helped him blend in with the other dads on the playground. From the back, he could pass for 40. From the front…well, let's just say the back was more forgiving.

His mother adjusted well to American life—she spoke with a faint brogue and was a certified Howard Stern fangirl. She was the one who took him to Yankees games and beach outings, fueling his lifelong love for both. (To this day, the man would probably renew his vows at Yankee Stadium if they offered wedding packages.)

And since he was basically corned beef and Guinness with legs, Mama from Manila came to the rescue bearing eggs that offered hope of dark hair and just enough mystery to make the family tree interesting.

But the biggest injustice of his childhood? Neither of his parents drove. Not even a learner's permit between them. He used to ask (often and dramatically) why, of all the billions of people in the world, these two non-drivers had to meet, fall in love, and create a child. Where was St. Patrick when you needed him??

Fate, with its penchant for comedy, made sure he spent 32 years as a New York City bus driver. Yes, the man who once resented relying on cabs and kind relatives (chauffeurs by blood obligation, not by choice) grew up to drive people who probably have parents who didn't drive either. (He actually wanted to be an accountant, but that's a story deserving its own paragraph.)

He has one sibling: a brother, three years his senior, who is a CPA somewhere in Westchester. So naturally, when it came time to pick a college major, my husband did not choose accounting; originality was at stake. Instead, he went with Computer Science which he quickly discovered was not his happy place. So I gladly let him handle the family bookkeeping so he could romance the receipts while I enjoyed spending freely.

Life doesn't always follow a map. But somehow, he found his route.

The bitter storm pushed
hard, but it gently handed us
the sweetest story.

BABY FROM THE BLIZZARD

O ur son's due date was March 11. But on a bone-chilling February morning, contractions barged in uninvited. Really? I thought. Couldn't this baby wait for spring? Or at least a day without frostbite warnings?

With a snowstorm on the way, my husband, in all his wisdom, made an "executive decision": a two-hour round-trip to the Bronx to fetch his mother. Apparently, childbirth could wait, but childcare negotiations could not. So I stayed home, pacing and contracting, waiting for him to get back. And during those long hours, I muffled my screams like I was auditioning for a horror film: on mute. The last thing I needed was to traumatize our girls into swearing off childbirth or Googling surrogacy before middle school.

When we finally made it to the hospital, no epidural was necessary. I was nearly fully dilated. What followed was a marathon of pushing, breathing, and more pushing until finally, the star of the show was born.

He looked like he'd been stuffed inside my womb for far too long. His cheeks bulged like a chipmunk at an all-you-can-eat nut buffet. But no, we didn't name him Alvin, Simon, or Theodore.

Despite arriving nearly a month ahead of schedule, he weighed in at 8 pounds and 14.5 ounces.

Doctors traded theories to explain why a baby born so soon looked ready for the wrestling ring. Mine was simpler (and probably closer to the truth): eight months of overeating, with maybe a few bonus years on the side.

Life follows its own schedule. But, we didn't care. Our son was prematurely perfect.

We weren't quack builders.
Our pride still peeks over
the fence of every missing
screw and every burst of our
children's laughter.

BUILDER, DONE THAT

We've all heard about gender role swaps. In our household, we had that occasionally. Not sure exactly how I turned out handy and DFDB… well, let's just say, he's got two hands.

The backyard looked like it was begging for a playset. So we ordered the classic combo of swings, gliders, trapeze rings, and a slide. A 165-pound box arrived with a thousand cheering nuts and bolts in tow. DFDB opened the box, very manly hands and all, and pulled out an instruction manual that looked more like a nuclear reactor blueprint.

His freckles retreated in fear as he passed it to me. We looked at each other, nodded like apprentices in need of courage, and agreed to start bright and early the next day.

Bright and early came. I was Foremama, assigning posts for this family project. DFDB was in charge of the big pieces (posts, beams, anything longer than six inches). The oldest was delegated to reading the steps and laying out the tools like an operating room nurse. The middle one matched the little parts to the pictures in the brochure. And our youngest—only six months old—watched intently from his stroller.

After eight hours, two and a half meals, bottle feedings, too many snack breaks, and a few unnecessary rest periods, we stared nervously at our "masterpiece" while several screws sat untouched in the box. After convincing ourselves those were just extras the manufacturer had tossed in, we let the kids test the fruit of our labor. And it prevailed!

Maybe he felt left out during the family construction activity, so the moment he learned what a Philips screwdriver was, our son was right beside me for every IKEA build. By the time he hit high school, I happily relinquished my hard hat and toolbox.

I later heard that Code 99 in stores is the discreet alert for a missing child. Code 66 in our house was the not-so-secret signal that an adult would always go missing: toolbox in, DFDB out.

Words are like wildflowers.

They grow everywhere, but

we only pick the ones closest

to our hearts.

DAD ON THE PAD

(ELF ON THE SHELF 1.0)

Several years before Elf on the Shelf became a Christmas tradition, I had my own version: "Dad on the Pad." No doll on a ledge, just index cards taped around the house, a two-year-old hunter on the prowl, and me—a mother hoping the game would sharpen his mind, tire his legs, and soothe my soul.

I wrote short words that were the most meaningful to him: "dad," "mom," "ball", and taught him to read them. Then the hunt began. "Get me Dad!" I'd call, and off he went—a determined Elmer Fudd with his sippy cup, examining walls and cabinets like a home inspector on a deadline. Just when he thought he had the map memorized, I'd move the cards around. Some sneaky planning went into making sure this three-foot recruit didn't get to employ his shortcuts. I'd also change one letter in the word to make sure he was really looking at it closely:

"dad" had his alter ego "dud"

"mom" and her British twin "mum"

"ball" didn't mind letting "bell" join in

And the bonus? He hit his 10k daily stepitas (c'mon, he's got short legs) before preschoolers even knew what a Fitbit was.

I'm not sure it taught him how to read, but I know he'll learn that sometimes the words we ask for are really meant for someone else to discover life's lessons scattered along the way.

You can smile, knowing what
you've been missing is safely
waiting to snap back
into place.

PIECE AND QUIET

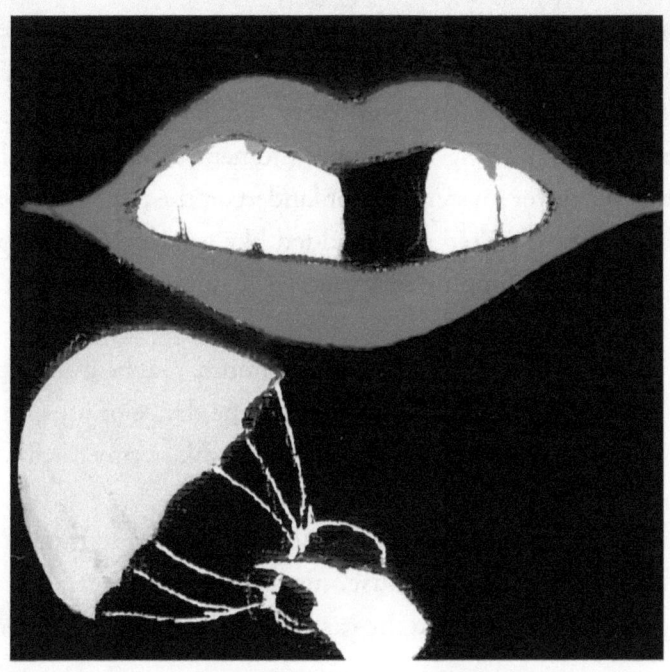

We decided our three-year-old was ready for a challenge, so I brought home an Arthur cartoon puzzle: 65 pieces. Too ambitious? Probably. But this was pre-Google parenting, when instinct and the store's educational toy aisle doubled as our guide in child rearing.

We thought the living room puzzle would be a quiet activity. The box promised 65 pieces of wholesome, educational calm.

Wholesome? Sure.

Educational? Definitely.

Calm? Well…

I dropped five pieces in the center as a starter kit. In my mind, this was a "Montessori meets Martha Stewart" moment. My own culinary puzzle was waiting in the kitchen, so after that, it was every man (okay, every toddler) for himself, and every mother praying for a quiet moment of reflection while tasting whatever mystery dinner landed on the table that night.

At first, he poked and prodded like a scientist, staring at the wavy edges, flipping each piece as if clues would appear on the back.

Eventually—maybe a couple of hours, maybe a couple of days, who knows—he did it! We did the dance of joy and let the puzzle sit proudly on the coffee table, like a tiny cardboard Mona Lisa, waiting to impress Dad.

The next morning, I expected him to parade it proudly to DFDB, demand applause, maybe even a congratulatory piggy-back ride. Instead, he casually mixed up all the pieces.

Just scattered them like Cheerios out of the box. Did I just raise a saboteur? An anarchist? Or worse: an anti-IKEA shopper?

Before my cortisol could hit cruising altitude, he surprised me. No tears, no regrets. He simply got to work again, moving faster this time. Each piece slipped in as if it had memorized its spot. He wasn't overwhelmed by the mess, he was fueled by it. He was confident like a seasoned traveler stuffing a carry-on after a random airport inspection, every piece snapping back into place with precision.

That's when I realized the real puzzle wasn't on the table. It was in his little head. He was building mastery and Arthur was his sidekick in this quest. Every free fall ended with that dramatic landing exactly where it should be.

And me? I was learning the quieter half of parenting: that somehow the victory isn't in the finished product but in the redo, the repeat, the relentless expectation that the picture will form again.

It struck me that family life is the puzzle that never stays finished. You celebrate the picture one night, only to wake up to scattered pieces and the quiet faith to rebuild.

Backpacks connect the home
to the classroom, the present
to the future. They're a
child's most faithful
companion.

BACKPACKS TO THE FUTURE

We enrolled him in a pre-K class for 4-year-olds, conveniently tucked in a church basement. A five-minute walk for us, a giant leap for his social life.

It was a cooperative school, which meant parents had to help out twice a month (a setup most were happy to comply with.) Well, most. There's always that one mother on the "less" side of helpful.

The setup was a healthy mix of "micro-academia" and playtime, indoors and out. His ABCs and numbers were spot-on. They had arts and crafts, songs, writing, drawing—basically what we did at home, except now he had 24 other kids fighting him for crayons and attention. A mini version of the real world they'd face in about 20 years.

Snack time arrived like clockwork. The POD (Parents on Duty) handled (bought and served) the munchies. Pepperidge Goldfish reigned supreme: neat, crunchy, pseudo-healthy. Capri Sun, with its exotic flavors and dangerously squeezable pouch, was demoted. We stuck to the all-American, less-accident-prone apple juice in Tetra Paks. (It secretly broke my heart, because the other one was my favorite, a tropical fruit nostalgia from you-know-where.)

Story time came next, an attempt to suppress the sugar surge. Kids plopped on the rug, waiting for the teacher to read. Meanwhile, parents began clean-up. I was relieved it wasn't part of our contract to take turns at the reading mat. I didn't need complaints that my non-native English speaker narration disrupted *Green Eggs and Ham*. Honestly, my accent was barely detectable. Well, it was virtually absent when I did sign language.

Then came playground release: children scattering like inmates set free for their daily dose of Vitamin D. They zipped down slides with glee, as if their buttocks had been greased with ghee. Watching the little ones play Ring Around the Rosie was fun to watch. Although it would've been pants-splitting comedy to see the parents join in and enjoy their failed attempts to get up with poise after the "we all fall down."

By day's end, the teacher-apprentices had every Lego piece back in custody, every rogue grain of sand recaptured, and backpacks (the silent couriers of daily stories) stuffed like evidence bags—no memo or artwork left behind.

During my "volunteer" shifts, I noticed something about him: he was a stickler for rules. He meticulously followed every one of the teacher's instructions like he'd been briefed by the Department of Justice. Was it fear of being reprimanded or were early principles already sprouting? I could almost hear the manila folders rhythmically opening and closing in his head. Structure didn't scare him; if anything, he scared the living daylights out of it.

No complaints here. Clearly, we didn't need to budget for bail money in the future, just his educational fund.

Maybe sometimes we send them out to be carefree with other kids, only to discover that order and fun can share the same sandbox.

The fridge door displayed
the true star—the lighthouse
waiting for its moment
to guide.

FRIDGE OVER
TROUBLED MARKER

Every day, he came home with truckloads of artwork. His backpack looked like the Salvation Army had accepted donations from starving artists who'd finally traded their dreams for a box of donuts.

Now, I wasn't one of those moms who slapped everything on the fridge like it was a gallery opening. If his work didn't reflect the effort and skill I knew he had the potential to bring to life, it didn't make it to the Hollywood Squares section of the refrigerator. WHAT? WHY WOULD I DO THAT?

Don't get me wrong; I acknowledged every single piece. But this Mama treating everything he made like it belonged in the MoMA wouldn't teach him to assess his own work. I didn't hand him a checklist. He had to figure it out on his own. Maybe the paper was stained, maybe there were too many erasures, maybe his name wasn't written clearly. Maybe it just wasn't.

And those kiddie Basquiat creations that made the cut? They weren't just vibrant exhibits on our fridge door—they were lighthouses guiding him away from the shallow waters of mediocrity and toward the open sea of excellence.

Small and squeaky often
echoes the loudest in a
child's heart.

I PAWS FOR A REPLY

First, a quick rewind. It began with my sisters. Both of them had pets when we were growing up: a poodle and a Japanese Spitz. I saw their four-pawed sponsored bundle of joy and chores. 'Twas a quick lesson for me to find happiness elsewhere.

Our kids never begged for furry, four-legged pets. Not once. Yes, we were as surprised as anyone. (I convinced myself my genes had nothing to do with it.)

The desire came from us. My husband and I believed that a "complete" household wasn't just walls and people: it needed the quiet company of little creatures. Quiet and little. That was the deal.

When the time came to open our doors, our choices were obvious. His Bronx childhood had been equally low on paws and whiskers. He had a bird, a turtle, and one surprisingly resilient rooster (which, in retrospect, he later insisted might have been a turkey). So we set the parameters for our own household zoo: a goldfish, a hermit crab, and a hamster.

People say pets have countless positive effects on children. I agree completely. We felt like true winners for giving our kids *pet care lite*: the non-roaming creatures that didn't demand housecleaning, leash training, or emotionally charged vet visits. It was one more family dynamic where everyone (human and non-human) got exactly what they needed from each other. And best of all? No one had to notify the ASPCA.

Well, except maybe that one time we smuggled a fishbowl into a hotel during vacation. Not our proudest felony.

They've since flown the nest. The oldest one now has both cats and dogs. Our middle child has a tortoise. And the reason for this book? He has a couple of not-so-needy plants, the ones that survive just fine as long as you occasionally remember they exist.

Sometimes the best lessons in responsibility aren't about what you're willing to take on, but about knowing exactly what you're not. Which might explain why he tends to plants instead of pets: a drama-free choice that proves he can nurture life…the kind that only demands what he's willing to give.

Monsters can be gentle when
they're wrapped up in their
own fear.

GENTLE MONSTER

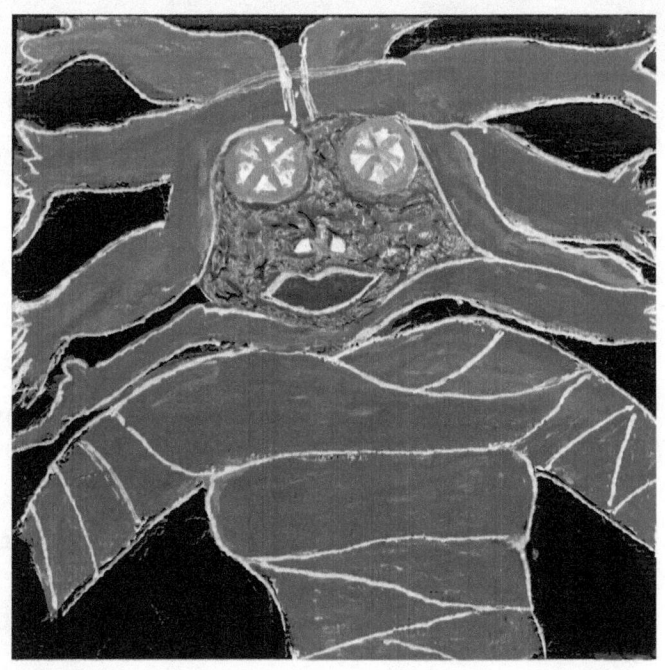

My son and I had a running tradition: scary movies together, lights off, popcorn reliably burnt. The twist? Even in my "tender" 40s (and 50s, if we're being honest), I was the one covering my eyes at suspenseful moments while he hid under a blanket like a pocket-sized monk in a pitch-black monastery. By his teens, the blanket retired and the throw pillow became his new shield.

Most moms I knew treated fear like mold: one exposure and the whole child would have to be thrown out.

Who needs nightmares, trauma, bed-wetting, and therapy bills? Well, I agreed with Robert Frost* and took the road less traveled. I figured shared goosebumps trumped any potential consequences. Reckless? Maybe. Lucky? Very.

When a movie left us more rattled than we bargained for, our therapy was simple: dig up a Disney classic. Like the ginger that comes with sushi, it cleansed the palate—this time, our fragile mental state. Goodbye monsters, hello princesses. Snow White never looked so reassuring.

Captions were non-negotiable (my ears grew up elsewhere). But secretly, I pretended they doubled as spelling drills. Those spooky subtitles turned out to be a warm-up act for the Korean dramas and Bollywood marathons he devoured later.

And here's the twist: the same boy who once hid under blankets went skydiving once for fun. No fairy-tale reset button

---

* **Robert Frost**—*an American poet frequently cited by parents right before making decisions their own mothers would not approve of.*

for me, just the seven dwarfs pounding on my heart while he free-fell from 10,000 feet.

Fear doesn't always stay the villain. It may be what makes you want to shut your eyes until it begs you to finally open them wide and let go.

The world presents the
buttons—we press the ones
that get us to the next round.

SUPER MAMA BROS.

Picture this: my kids are on the edge of their seats, cheering me on as I defeat Bowser and finally save the Princess. Not watching their own gameplay but watching mine.

Yes, it's fair to say that when I opened the road for our son to play video games, it came paved and with no speed bumps in sight.

Parents love their warnings. Video games will melt your brain. Friendships? Gone. Future? Doomed. Sure. And yet, here's my story.

I grew up (if that's what you call ages eleven to twenty-four) on Pong, Space Invaders, Breakout, and my ride-or-die: Super Mario Bros. My parents never told me to stop playing. Maybe I knew when to quit or maybe they were secretly watching what they never had as kids.

So when the time came for me to be the parent, I passed down this rare gift: the ability to enjoy screen time guilt-free. No timers. No lectures. Just HD joy and sheer disbelief that I'd been allowed into their world. And I didn't even knock.

It turned out the best way to teach my kids about winning wasn't a pep talk. It was letting them watch me do it. And the kicker? I didn't have to start with basics. We went straight to strategy and put The Art of War to shame. Sometimes your kids show up already suited up for the mission, and they just need you to show that victory may not come right away, but when you're being cheered on, it feels as though you've already won…a thousand times over.

INTERMISSION: THE CONSOLE YEARS

The Super Nintendo system needed an upgrade. It was more than ten years old and definitely no spring chicken.

At six, he unwrapped a brand-new PlayStation 2 complete with Ratchet & Clank, Men in Black, and the latest Madden NFL.

And every time a new system hit the shelves—Xbox, PlayStation 3, Nintendo Switch—it somehow materialized under the tree. (Santa got credit for a couple of years.)

Some parents hand down wisdom; I handed over my credit card to secure my son's next level.

BREAKING: DAD HAS ENTERED THE CHAT

Permission granted, even though he's never held a joystick in his life. His official statement? Turns out video games aren't just entertainment. They teach our son the rules of MLB, NFL, NHL & NBA, no coach required. Video games get credit for teaching him sports better than ESPN ever could.

Hands-on Mama. Hands-off Dad. Together, we gave him the whole game.

Power can be harnessed
in many ways. But the
energy that flows freely is
unstoppable.

CHORES BE GONE

We've always been told that children need chores so they grow into responsible adults. In our house, that theory showed up late, looked around, and left without making eye contact. If responsibility was a guest, it ghosted us with an Irish goodbye. I suspected there had to be a nouvelle idée—one that promised the same results without blood pressure spikes and power struggles.

Take out the trash? Wash the dishes? Make the bed? Those were battles I had no interest in fighting. Why let the day—mine and theirs—get ruined by routine tasks? At best, nagging would make them do it. So I'd lose my voice in a non-karaoke activity and still be unsure what I had trained them for.

So I swapped daily chores for creative duties—**creduties**, as I lovingly called them.

The task? Entertain the family.

And since smartphones hadn't yet marched in like the big shots they believed they were, I handed them our trusty Sony camcorder. They took turns being reporters, magicians, and pop stars. It was like a parenting x-ray, best viewed with buttered popcorn. Watching those tapes wasn't just fun; they were unexpectedly revealing. We learned:

What they noticed.

What they dreamed of.

What they believed the future might look like.

Of course, the end of each show turned into evidence recovery: scarves-turned-capes, kitchen whisks repurposed as microphones, and my bamboo chopsticks moonlighting as magician's wands. A small price to pay and it kept my investigative instincts sharp.

Not every night was a "big" production. Sometimes we lingered at the dinner table long after the food was gone, turning it into an impromptu "Make Me Laugh" segment. Our little boy fought hard to outwit his older sisters because the least funny one would be sentenced to my imaginary Humor 101 class.

Looking back, missing the mop doesn't mean ditching discipline. Those nightly jokes, living room newscasts, and amateur magic shows taught them presence, timing, and the courage to speak up. No, they don't fold towels like a five-star hotel linen attendant. But they can hold an audience, read a room, and pivot when life forgets the script.

And in case anyone's keeping score: none of them do dishes to this day. The oldest lives with her husband who so willingly handles sink duty, the middle one maintains an arsenal of disposable cutlery like she's preparing for an apocalypse-themed picnic, and our boy eats out like a Michelin inspector trying to meet quota.

They clearly took my freedom-from-chores philosophy to heart. But in defense of my nonconformist curriculum: we have a writer, an artist, and a software engineer all excelling in their fields—while owning dishwashers that, like them, are free from washing duties.

Tupperware can wait, talent can't.

The heart is a muscle meant

to grow stronger with

every pain.

But some losses weaken its

will to try again.

JAMSTER'S ADDRESS

The summer he was ten, my son had one pet that was truly his own—a hamster he named Jamster. The goldfish had been communal, but Jamster was his. His companion. His joy.

That day, I picked him up from baseball camp, and like always, the first thing he did when we got home was rush upstairs to see his pet. A minute later, I heard him screaming Jamster's name. I knew instantly why.

There's no way to cushion a child's grief. Your child hurting is a dagger to your chest that twists deeper with every tear. All I could do was lift Jamster's little body and place him in a box: small, sturdy, almost as if it had been made for him. On the outside was my name and address. I told my son, "He'll never get lost this way."

We buried Jamster beneath the sweet cherry tree in our backyard. We covered him with soil, whispered our prayer through sobs, and said goodbye. To this day, every blossom and piece of fruit reminds me that beneath this tree rests a tiny life that once made my son feel less alone.

He never asked for another pet.

So I let their story stay pristine, untouched by levity.

Here rests a gentle soul, mourned by a tiny heart.

He completed the puzzle. I labeled it "Finished."
We were both three in our own way.

DFDB handed him his first bat at two. Four years later, he
returned the favor by showing him the swing.

I could hear Josh Groban in the background. 'You raise me up...' The fence, the playset, and I all took it literally.

If your friends jumped off a plane, would you?
Forgot to mention it was rhetorical.

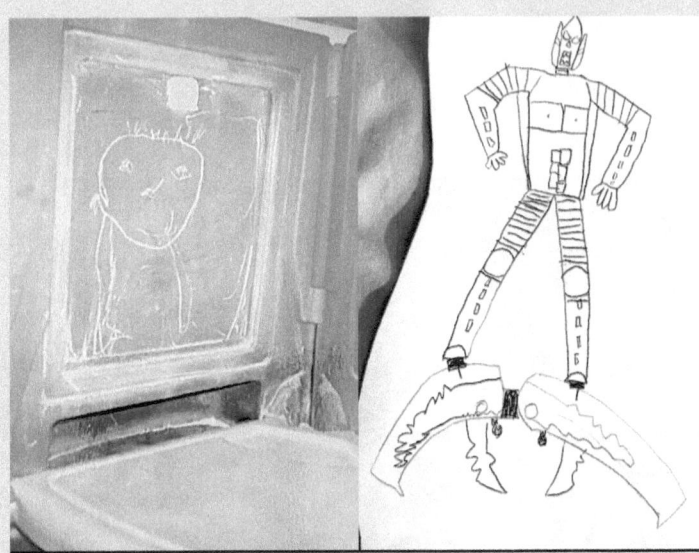

A self-portrait at three and the Green Goblin at six. Some kids pick crayons , he picked a hero and a villain.

Costumes by me. Props by the kitchen. Two plumbers, one sink—perfectly sinkronized.

63

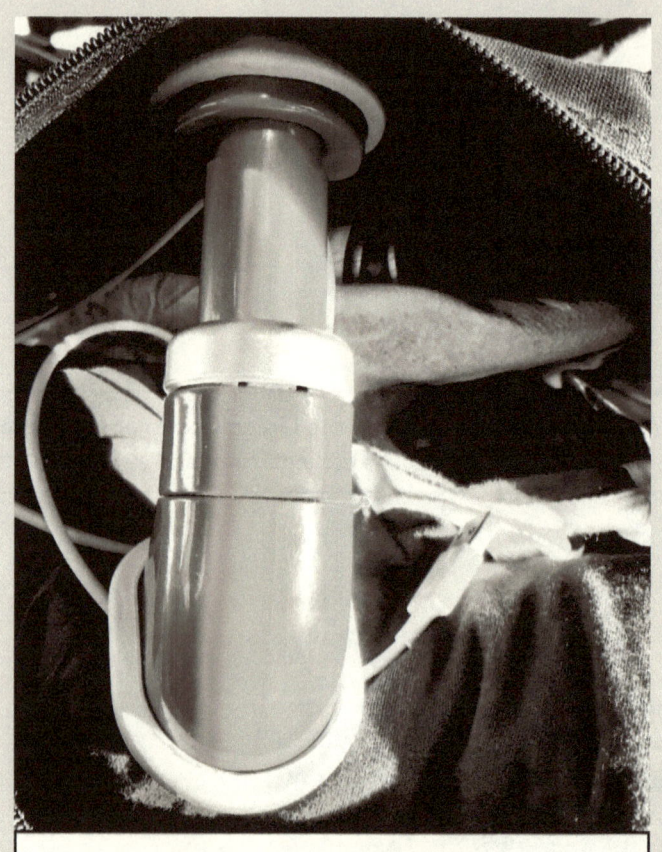

They say beauty is skin-deep,
But I can't help but weep.
And from my son not even a peep,
So TSA says the chin exerciser is mine to keep.
—LaGuardia Gate Poetry

High school graduation party. That's what friends
are for: dunking.
At least, for the brave ones. The rest:
Dunkin' Do Nots.

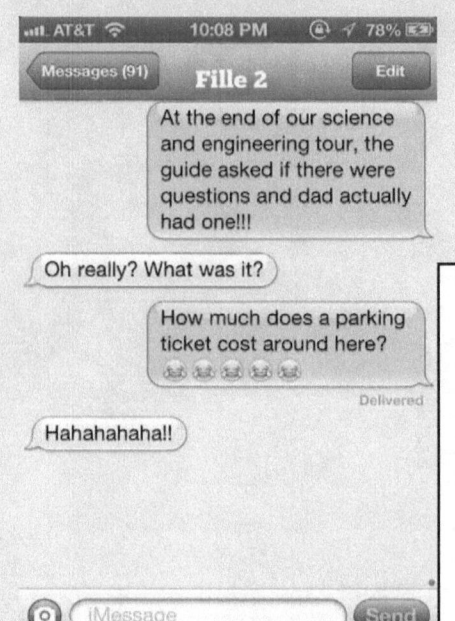

> At the end of our science and engineering tour, the guide asked if there were questions and dad actually had one!!!

> Oh really? What was it?

> How much does a parking ticket cost around here? 😂😂😂😂😂

Delivered

> Hahahahaha!!

Harvard Visitas—an annual event for newly admitted students and their parents to visit campus before they enroll. They encouraged questions. I passed. DFDB did not. I almost passed out.

Top Ten Students got to choose a pose and a quote. He added extra human props.

This is Annenberg Hall. Harvard freshmen eat here. I came, I saw, I cornered a spot for the photo op. (A respectful nod to Julius Caesar, also a lover of a good entrance. And let's leave his departure out of this.)

Dad,
I don't know what the card says, either.

Y nos llenan el corazón
con un infinito amor.

FELIZ DÍA DEL PADRE
a un papá muy admirado.

Thanks for being a cool dad. You'll have to wait until my first check for a gift. Hopefully the fact that I'm working suffices for now.

Your 2nd favorite son,

DFDB didn't know Spanish or any second son. Since then, he has begun Duolingo in search of answers.

The buzz isn't always noise.
It can be the music that lets
you dance while admiring
the flower.

TV OR NOT TV

(SHAKESPEARE MUST BE PROUD)

I'm padding myself with bubble wrap before easing you into this one. Remember, I grew up in Manila. We were your standard middle-class family, but by some cultural and economic fluke, we had maids. Yes, plural. And they were live-in helpers, not the kind who vanished at 5 p.m., leaving you to fend for yourself until morning.

Both my parents worked, so we'd come home to a spotless house, after-school merienda*, and dinner practically ready the moment the breadwinners (primary and backup) walked through the door. The only adults around during those purgatorial hours were the hired help. Between arriving home and dinner, we'd do homework with the TV on. Always. I'd be scribbling answers between popping Chippy chips (think Doritos in their awkward adolescence) and sipping Fanta Orange. No one (kids or adults) thought anything was amiss.

Yes, you read that right: homework and TV, coexisting in what I can only describe as chaotic harmony. And somehow, the principal never learned my name (having a long, uncommon one might have helped a little).

Now that I've softened you with this confession, here's the kicker: the same "mind-blowing" practice had a New York version minus the Chippy, the Fanta, and, sadly, the maids. Not sure why I wasn't distracted by the so-called "idiot box" (a term the older generation tossed around like watermelon

---

* **Merienda**—an imported Spanish tradition Filipinos kept after 300 years of colonial hosting duties. We sent the colonizers home but kept the snacks.

seeds), but apparently, my kids inherited the same mutant gene.

Maybe the TV acted like white noise, filtering out bigger distractions. Or maybe it was just the hypnotic comfort of background chatter. Either way, the homework got done—done well, in fact. No school calls that started with a sigh, no complaints about shoddy submissions. And CPS**? Never once knocked on our door.

Because sometimes the secret isn't eliminating distractions, but teaching kids to work through them. So when life gets distractingly noisy, they can still focus and forge ahead... straight into Cambridge's coveted corridors.

** **CPS**—*Child Protective Services, the American agency that shows up when your parenting style steps into the "ma'am, we need to talk" arena.*

When the mask finally comes off, the morning after reveals principle, fully unwrapped.

PARTY HATS OFF
TO YOU

Call it a Twilight Zone moment, but have you ever heard of a mom offering a no-school day? Think of it as the parental version of the corporate "use it or lose it" vacation policy.

So, when the day after Halloween fell on a school night, I was ready to call the school and report my child "out sick." Not hacking, fever-ridden illness: but a spirit-was-willing, body-just-couldn't-do-it day. And even more surprising than my eagerness to mastermind and participate in this ploy was the fact that this unicorn offer was turned down. Every. Single. Time.

Look, this wasn't about raising a slacker. This was about teaching life skills in real time. If corporate execs can call it a mental health day, why can't a kid cash in the same perk, especially after the high-risk investment in a ridiculous costume and the door-to-door solicitation of unvetted candy givers?

I thought I was offering him a taste of a tiny rebellion, sugar-coated in maternal logic. But maybe he was flexing harder than I was: by choosing obligation over temptation, and showing me that not every sweet offer needs to be unwrapped. Turns out, that was the only treat I didn't see coming.

I raised a kid who could resist hooky. Proud? Yes. Offended? Absolutely.

Some lessons bloom in chaos,

just like warning cones can

still hold flowers.

WHEN SADLY
MET HURRY

text from your child filled with a gazillion exclamation points and not a single smiley emoji is the universal code for: "Mom, I'm in trouble."

As we all know, the annual science fair is the school's subtle way of "encouraging" parental involvement. Just enough to know the title of the experiment and foot the bill for the trifold board.

At around 5 p.m., I was informed that the project was due the next day. I asked (calmly) how far we were from the finish line. I pretended not to panic. Then came the bowed head, followed by a whisper so angelic it could disarm any mother:

"I haven't even started yet."

I had every right to scream, to summon an apoplectic storm. But I didn't.

I didn't lash out.

I didn't guilt-trip.

And I think that was an empathetic moment.

Why? Because many moons ago, I was that child.

I still remember my parents quietly finishing my project the night before it was due. No scolding. No shaming. Just their fingers working fast and hard to beat the deadline. I still don't know what possessed me to end up in that last-minute scramble. But what stayed with me was the Golden Rule of parenting: *Give your kids the tender moments your parents gave you.*

So, we went into triage mode. There would be no shopping trip, no fancy display, no miracle supplies. Just whatever we could scrape together in the house. I found the old Polaroid camera (surely we could use pictures for something). We raided the kitchen, the laundry room, and maybe even the sock basket. The experiment? A blindfolded smell test. Food, feet—nothing was off limits.

To the best of my questionable knowledge, this was the hypothesis for our instant science project:

Advancing age is expected to reduce sensitivity to odors and accuracy in identifying them, as measured by a structured smell test.

And in layman's poetic terms:

> Sticks and stones may break your bones,
> And the hair in your old noses
> Won't let you smell the roses.

Our family of five became the test subjects. Then I sent him and his sister door-to-door on our short block, staging a kind of springtime Halloween. Instead of collecting candy, they tricked the eyes-covered, nose-wide-open neighbors into guessing the mystery scent. Every participant had to smell the full lineup: alcohol (not the fun kind), a tuna sandwich, Bengay (to help the older whiffers—no way the young'uns knew what this was), and a few nose-friendly items. Everyone had a smell of a time, and somehow we sniffed together enough "data" to fill the trifold.

Whether it was guilt over throwing me into a state of cardio-panic or his own realization that work done in a hurry looked undeniably like it, we never got stuck in a science fair traffic nightmare again.

Sometimes the best lessons aren't in the experiment, but in the grace we choose under pressure.

Parenting works best when
one hand catches what life
hurls while the other stays
open for whatever wants to
take flight.

PITCHES & VERVE

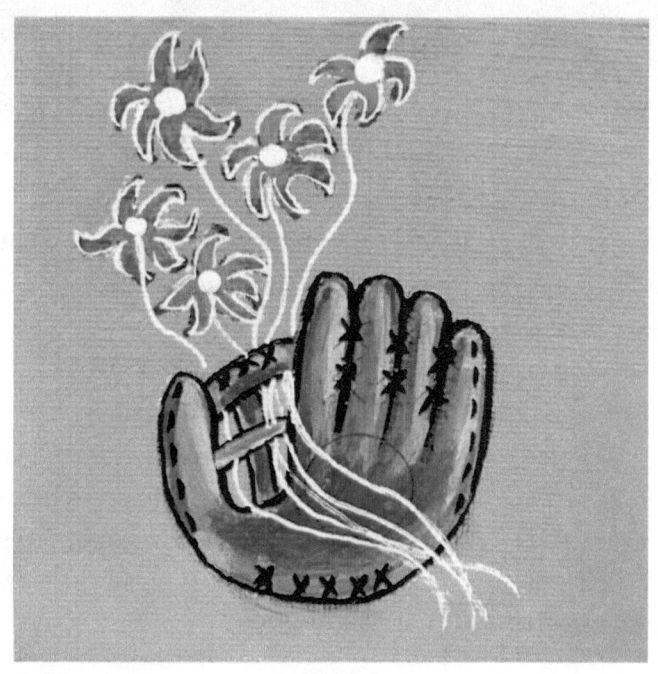

Splitting parenting duties wasn't rocket science, but let's be honest, it was never a true 50/50 split. Sports? Fully his department. He got our son into T-ball at age four. A lifelong Yankees fan was born, molded, and set for what he hoped would be uninterrupted years of baseball obsession.

Then came peewee football.

That one, I never quite approved of. No helmet, pad, or athletic cup (NASA—engineered or Kryptonian) could calm my nerves. The thought of my child being tackled before he'd even lost all his baby teeth did not thrill me. I found myself breathing like I was back in labor: starting with those slow, controlled belly breaths they teach you in Lamaze, trying to stay relaxed. But the second the tackling and piling began, I was right back in the hee-hee-hoo phase of active contractions, clutching an invisible epidural.

After a few weeks of that emotional rollercoaster, I skipped right past shallow breathing, went full delirious-mama mode, and slammed that don't-torture-me-anymore buzzer like it owed me child support.

Mission accomplished.

Father and son soon settled into their baseball groove. Little League became a major fixture in our lives for the next nine years. Our son cycled through outfielder, catcher, and eventually pitcher. My husband would always rave about how beautiful his little athlete's swing was. I assume in their world, that was high praise.

Meanwhile, my domain was anything school-related that didn't involve sweating or scoreboards. I was the queen of over-the-top projects, pushing creativity like a back-alley sequined craft dealer high on solvent fumes. In second grade, he had to do a report on a U.S. President. While his classmates showed up with a photo glued on an oak tag, we rolled in with a 15-inch 3D puppet of Grover Cleveland. Because…obviously.

My personal favorite? The 100th Day of School project. Most kids brought in poster boards covered in 100 pieces of pasta, cotton balls, or Skittles. We went for shock and awe. One year, we submitted a giant open mouth with 100 clothes-pins as teeth: 50 on top, 50 on bottom. The following year, it was a massive eyeball with 100 lashes made from garbage twist ties.

In hindsight, I'm not sure why we never made a face with 100 zits. That would've been our pièce de résistance—or a cautionary poster at a dermatologist's office.

In the end, our divided labor wasn't about balance. It was about rhythm. DFDB brought the cleats and the bat; I came armed with googly eyes and a glue gun. Somewhere between his disciplined moves and my wild creations, our little boy got the best of both worlds: pinpoint pitching and immense imagination.

What's locked up isn't always danger. Sometimes, it's simple indulgence.

GOLDILOCKS

Most people reserve lockable doorknobs for bathrooms. But I've always been an equal-opportunity installer, so I put them on every bedroom door. Personally. With my own two hands and the ever-dependable Black & Decker drill.

My kids thought I was training for a job at Home Depot. DFDB had questions, but he knew the saying: *handy wife, hands-off life.*

Why? Because I couldn't relax in my own bedroom without the assurance that "forgetful knockers" wouldn't accidentally waltz in. It wasn't that I was doing anything illegal or immoral (although the lock did make tweezing my eyebrows feel more oddly illicit). Maybe it's paranoia or just a simple aversion to surprises in any form.

And I wanted to share that secure feeling with everyone in our house. Let's be realistic: knocking is a courtesy, not a reflex.

If my kids felt like pulling ridiculous faces in the mirror or trying on outfits that made them look like backup dancers on a clearance budget, I wanted them to do it without fear of someone barging in.

So I gave them something rare: a private, lockable 9' x 12' kingdom where guests could never come unannounced. The lock wasn't just hardware bequeathed by a paranoid queen mother; it was a moat of security and freedom.

And in case of emergencies, everyone knew where the keys were kept.

Maybe sometimes the best gift you can give isn't the key to the world. It's the lock that lets someone make it their own.

Wide-awake moments
tend to mute the colors of
childhood's carefree spell.

THE TAMING OF
THE SNOOZE

Enforcing a sleep curfew is a nightly parenting ritual as old as bedtime stories, except in our household, where it's optional.

Because really, what's the point of lying in bed, staring at the ceiling, when your brain isn't ready for curtain call? I'd rather have the kids spend those hours doing something productive.

Our late-night "rules" only had two non-negotiables: no opening or closing the front door, and no cooking of any kind. Not because of fire hazards or safety concerns, mind you, but because I like my kitchen cleaned a certain way, and waking up to a greasy pan was not part of my morning vision board.

For as long as he was up for school on time and I didn't get a call from his teacher about him falling asleep in class, we were good. Remember the saying you give a hand, and they ask for an arm? In this case, you offer the arm while keeping the fist clenched.

In the end, curfews were never about clocks. They were about trust. About knowing when to unclench the fist and let the night teach its own lessons. And waking to the truth that discipline wears many disguises.

DAD ALERT:

The night was mine, but DFDB would rear his ugly, yet annoyingly luscious-haired head on weekends. No sleep-ins allowed. He was the weekend morning monster, an Awaken by Kraken routine rooted in his working world growing up.

By age eleven, he was up at 5:30, tossing newspapers before making it to class by eight. Sundays meant altar-boy duty at the 9 a.m. mass. By sixteen, he was pumping gas, not iron (which might explain his literal big head on a stick...body). Thanks to his sleep-deprived youth, the only luggage he carried into dadhood was his eye bags.

He may have been the little bus that could, but I was definitely the Manila jeepney that couldn't resist all the fun stops.

Turn things over and let the
magic work so you don't
have to.

WORK AND
PLEASE, DON'T

Dad from da Bronx has always been a believer in getting kids up and working the minute they hit high school. "That's how I was raised," he claimed, as if it were part of some sacred neighborhood creed. I, on the other hand, came from a family where working while in school wasn't even on the menu. You finished school first, then you got a good-paying job. End of story.

So, a dichotomy existed (ooh, look at me using a big word) between our opposing views on the "when" of entering the workforce. While I didn't vocally challenge his work-while-still-in-school mentality, I also didn't so much as lift my pinky to nudge the kids toward securing an after-school gig.

Our future Ivy attendee eventually landed his first work nest at clothing retailer American Eagle. Bronx Dad was finally appeased; I was...let's just say, not entirely popping champagne over it. Sure, you could argue that working teaches the value of money and the dignity of labor. And yes, you'd be right. But I've never been a believer in doing major things all at once.

It's like an all-in-one printer. Yes, it can scan, copy, and print, but none of it is particularly impressive. I wanted my child to focus on schoolwork, build lifelong friendships, and play the sports he loved without having to juggle shift schedules, scramble for coverage when a game ran late, or find the strength to call in sick when he was already down for the count. Those burdens, I figured, could wait until he actually entered the real world.

TALENT ALERT:

Our son proudly announced one evening that he had become the best shirt-folder at American Eagle. A title, I might add, that he awarded to himself with zero supporting witnesses. To this day, I've yet to see this legendary folding technique in action. Although, to be fair, his gift-wrapping skills are almost as good as mine. So either retail trained him...or our IKEA Batman-and-Robin academy handed him the cape and the scotch tape.

So, to work or not to work? The answer was simple: let work wait, so life could happen.

We roll out carry-ons
preloaded with things
eagerly waiting to turn into
memories—some endearing,
others requiring therapy.

RUSHIN' ROULETTE

I t started on a cruise. My carry-on was pulled aside, and security insisted I was smuggling in a suspicious set of pliers. Who in their right mind brings pliers on vacation? Well…I did. Except they weren't pliers at all: just a single hole puncher.

In my defense, I brought one every year. The cabin cards didn't come with holes for lanyards, and I was ahead of my time because eventually the cruise lines caught on. A room card with a hole was the Rolls Royce edition for kids. I wasn't about to let my son lose his card slipping in and out of those flimsy plastic sleeves. Call it overprotective, call it resourceful. I call it maternal foresight.

Since then, the real vacation countdown didn't begin at the first selfie spot but at security. That was where I secretly played my little game: carry-on roulette. No one knew which family member would be the unsuspecting courier until the alarms went off.

That holiday, our son got lucky (or unlucky, depending on your angle). His TSA-PreCheck ticket was no match for fate's humor. His bag was flagged, and out came the notorious contraband: my chin exerciser.

The agents didn't recognize it. I gave a quick demo, but their faces said, "Ma'am, you still have a double chin." Just as I was ready to surrender it, a female agent from another line walked over, broke into a grin, and confirmed my story. DFDB laughed, the kids cringed, and TSA remained unconvinced.

That's the roulette thrill—you never know when the souvenirs will show up: before the vacation or after.

Some lessons run on wheels,
others on will—and the road
rises up to meet them.

MY WILL, HIS WHEEL

Let's talk about that rite of passage to mobility freedom. Being able to drive on their own without the uncool adult in the car is probably the most coveted moment of 17-year-olds, hands down.

But as parents know too well, this teenage release from bondage comes with a hefty price tag. The turmoil (emotional, mental, physical) was brutal for me. Well, I anticipated it would be, so DFDB became the designated shock absorber for teaching all our kids how to drive. I may be the teacher, but driving is tightly braided in his genes.

I never rode in the car with our kids driving until they were all out of the house and off our car insurance policy. Others probably call it a show of no confidence, but I brand it as guaranteed immunity from anti-anxiety prescriptions.

DFDB has always been the default choice when an instructor/trainer/calmer mentor was needed for anything with wheels: rollerblades, bikes, cars. I only mastered one thing with wheels: the stroller. Here's the deal: I carried two of them for nine months and one for eight, so it was only fair (and perfectly logical) that he'd set them up for life's open roads.

I should also mention DFDB had (still has) the agility of a squirrel on espresso and the patience of a man watching grass grow. For these qualities I don't possess, I thank the universe for our family's wheel whisperer.

Because when it comes to handing over the keys, sometimes love means stepping aside, my will giving way to his wheel.

Letting go wasn't failure—it's
tossing the chip into the bowl
trusting the duck could swim.

LET THE TORTURE CHIPS FALL WHERE THEY MAY

Once again, Halloween found its way onto the hors d'oeuvre plate of our family story.

It was October 31st, and he was in our living room hanging out with friends. Laptop open, as usual. He could've been gaming, doing homework, or watching old videos, nothing unusual there. But I could not shake the anxiety bubbling in me, the kind that teeters between Urgent Care and full-on Emergency Room.

He was applying to Harvard's Restrictive Early Action program. The application was due November 1. And no matter how DFDB and I tried, we couldn't get an update on whether everything was done.

We probably had better luck getting a tracking report on an Uber Eats driver who got sick mid-delivery (strictly from illness, not from sneaking a fry—just to be clear).

I lingered in the kitchen, pretending to be busy while eavesdropping, hoping for any crumb of conversation related to his application. Then I heard it: the most nonchalant "done," followed by a brain-freeze-inducing "and send."

Edvard Munch's The Scream doesn't come close to my facial-twitching, eye-popping, jaw-in-free-fall reaction when that chilling word hit my ears.

Essay draft unseen.

Final copy sent.

Deadline met.

Dream put on hold.

The real test wasn't if I could help him craft the perfect essay. It was if I could let go and trust he didn't need me to.

He hit "send." I gently pressed "let go."

Because sometimes the hardest part of parenting isn't teaching them what to do—it's trusting they already know.

I won't paste his entire college essay here. That's his story to own. But I can share the part that stopped me in my tracks exactly as Harvard saw it:

"...to appease my own curiosity about LIFE—the single word we try to use to identify something so complex, ambiguous, and something that may be forever beyond what we can comprehend, which is what makes it so precious and extraordinary."

Additional grumbling moments:

Other milestones I never got to read before their grand debut:

1. His valedictory speech

2. His address as commencement speaker at his old high school ten years after he graduated

At this rate, requesting a draft of my eulogy (thirty years from now, allowing for extensions—both hair and lifespan) feels like a perfectly reasonable ask.

Some victories are meant to echo all the way across, and the heart jumps and spins to their rhythm.

THE VIEW FROM THE OTHER SIDE... OF MY HEART

I sometimes wonder if my son got into an Ivy League school because of me...or in spite of me. Oh, and let's not forget Dad from da Bronx, he at least had a cameo.

The truth? It's probably not one or the other. All the somewhat surprising choices, last-minute detours, and creative lessons came together into one unconventionally built but sturdy bridge. Unwavering. Somehow, he crossed it. Straight to Harvard.

When he looked back from the other side, he probably would've preferred just a smile and a wave. He should've known better. There we were, jumping up and down with a silly grin, and for the next four years, we dropped the H-bomb all wrapped in shameless joy and sealed with a bragging bow... on unsuspecting civilians.

Approximate tally:

- 1 Salvation Army bell ringer

- 1 Amazon delivery guy who definitely didn't ask

- 1 doctor + his 3 nurses

- 2 postmen (ours and our friend's in the next town)

- 30 airline passengers (give or take)

- >1,000 bystanders who must have overheard it

And not to forget the one guy at the ATM who made the mistake of making eye contact.

So he crossed the bridge, and we cheered too loudly. But if bridges could talk, they wouldn't hush us. They'd understand why joy echoes the loudest from the other side.

For all the unexpected
moments—thank you,
my son.

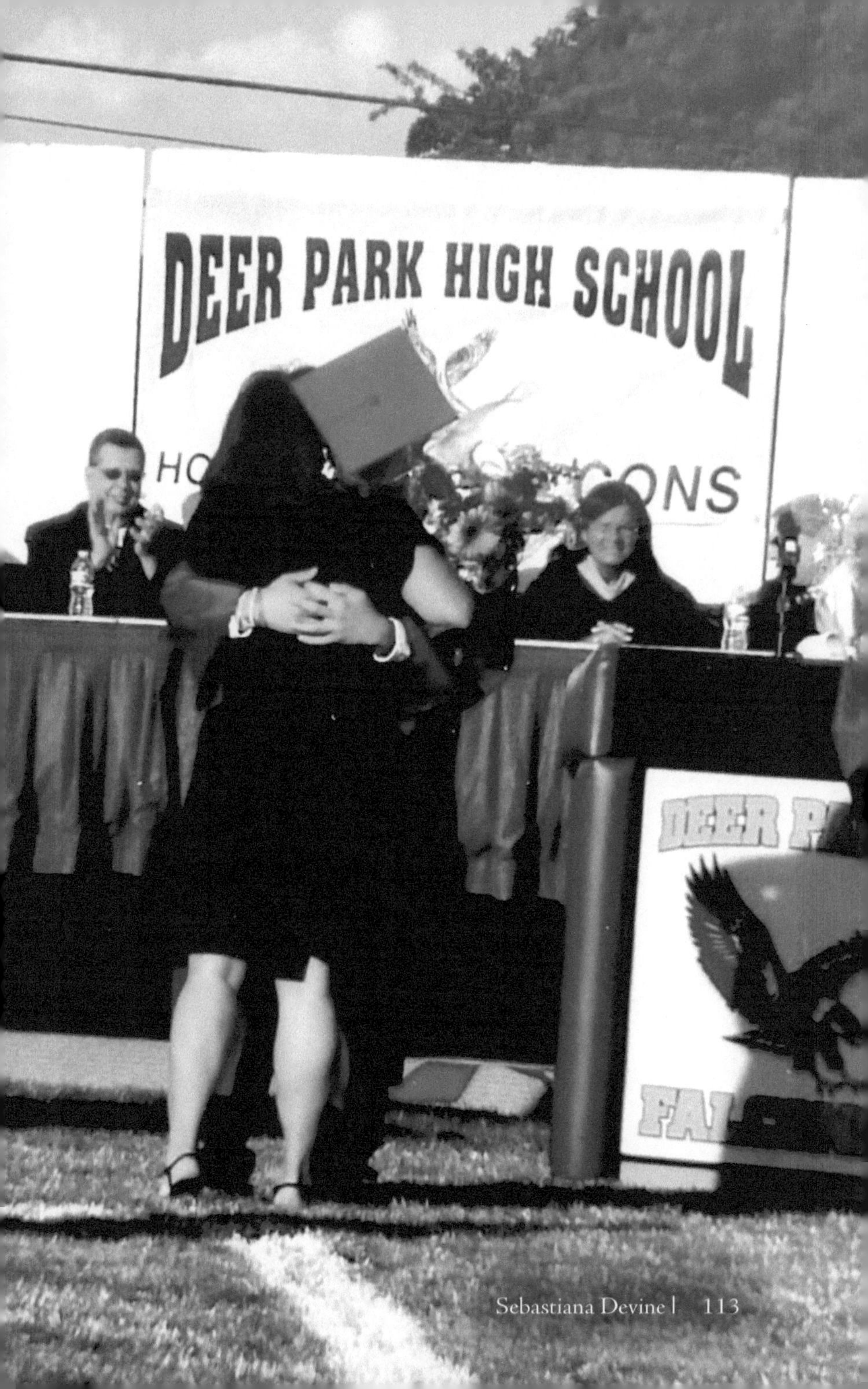
DEER PARK HIGH SCHOOL

SPRINKLES &
MIXED-INS

(LAISSEZ-FAIRE, BUT NOTICING EVERYTHING...OR NOT)

- Never enrolled in an *SAT prep class (no finger pointing necessary).

- Joined Cooks for Kids at the Ronald McDonald House (now, making Japanese fluffy pancakes just for kicks).

- Rapped while doing lab experiments (not revealing my source).

- Donated plasma at his high school blood drive and almost fainted (heroes are clueless sometimes).

- Picked the drums for his musical instrument (nah, too easy).

- Chose Italian for his foreign language (I suggested French).

- Fell while skateboarding; scraped his arm, didn't want me to know, and wore a sweater for 2 weeks...in the summer.

- Didn't eat a hamburger until middle school because he thought it had ham.

- Had to be carried to his room after falling asleep on the living room couch most nights (we capped it at 100 pounds).

- Painted his bedroom stadium red (was it a mood room?).

- Lost his pen in school almost every day (that's how DFDB got started collecting promo pens at events).

- Took the PSAT while running a fever. I didn't know; I was in Manila. DFDB was home—he didn't know either.

GLOSSARY OF SPRINKLES

- PSAT = the practice SAT, America's favorite stress appetizer

- SAT = the students' overcooked steak: tough

- DFDB= Dad from da Bronx, just to be clear

ACKNOWLEDGMENTS

I'm not entirely sure who wants to be acknowledged here…and who would rather remain safely unmentioned.

So let's keep this simple:

To those who helped, thank you.

To those who doubted, also thank you.

To those who would prefer not to be named, don't worry, no one really cares.

Parenting may include the whole village, but writing about it means leaving a few villagers out.

And to everyone else, you mattered more than you know.

I WINK, THEREFORE I JAM

To my Philosophy professors:

Thank you for every C+ so generously bestowed, even when I barely understood Descartes or Kant.

Should either of them roll in his grave after reading my quotes on parental wisdom, I'll take pride in knowing I finally moved someone.

KISMET

The artworks here were painted long before this book was even a thought.

Maybe this is proof that some stories and some art are destined to meet.

And when they finally did, they spoke in quotes that now belong to you.

Locked out on the first day of classes.

Yes, really.

That's his door. I took the photo on our first visit back, a reminder for both of us that the key was always meant to be his.

ABOUT THE AUTHOR

Sebastiana Devine is a mother who writes, paints, and parents with wit. She lives quietly in New York with her husband, as their three children have already spread their wings to other parts of the state.

"We don't call it an empty nest," she says. "It's a bird bath—where our kids can always come for a quick dip in Mom and Dad's wit and wisdom."

www.ingramcontent.com/pod-product-compliance
Lightning Source LLC
Chambersburg PA
CBHW020738130626
46554CB00006B/2044